leeches

The Gruesome Truth About

The Victorians

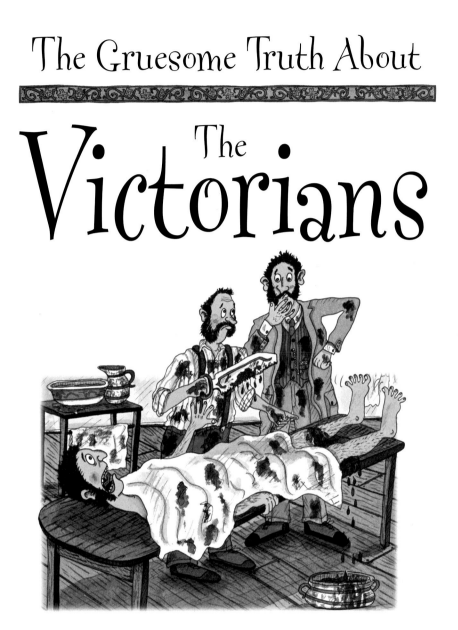

Written by

Jillian Powell

Illustrated by

Matt Buckingham

WAYLAND

First published in 2010 by Wayland

Text copyright © Wayland 2010
Illustration copyright © Matt Buckingham 2010

Wayland
338 Euston Road
London NW1 3BH

Wayland Australia
Level 17/207 Kent Street
Sydney NSW 2000

Editor: Victoria Brooker
Design: billybooks.co.uk
Consultant: Dr Paul Young, Lecturer in Victorian
Literature and Culture, University of Exeter

British Library Cataloguing in Publication Data
Powell, Jillian.
Gruesome truth about the Victorians.
1. Great Britain--History--Victoria, 1837-1901--Juvenile
literature. 2. Great Britain--Social life and customs--
19th century--Juvenile literature.
I. Title II. Victorians
941'.081-dc22

ISBN 978 0 7502 6135 7

Printed in China

Wayland is a division of Hachette Children's Books,
an Hachette UK company.
www.hachette.co.uk

Contents

The Vivacious Victorians

The Victorians lived in Britain under the rule of Queen Victoria (1837 – 1901). The Victorian age was a time of great inventions and discoveries. Explorers travelled overseas and brought back tales and treasures. The railway, photography, electric lighting and the telephone were invented.

▲ The Victorians gave us the first photographs of our ancestors.

The Penny Post was set up as the first reliable postal service for cards and letters. Even the Christmas card was invented by the Victorians!

▲ Queen Victoria's head appeared on penny coins and stamps.

▲ The telephone was invented by Alexander Graham Bell in 1875.

Gruesome truth

Those are some of the things that you probably already know about the Victorians, but in this book you'll find out the gory and grisly bits that no one ever tells you! Each double page will begin with a well-known FACT, before going on to tell you the **gruesome truth** about the Victorians. Look out for these features throughout the book – the answers are on page 32.

▼ Steam trains meant people could travel faster and further for work or holidays.

WHAT IS IT?
Guess the mystery object.

TRUE OR FALSE?
Decide if the statement is fact or fiction.

Homes and Hygiene

FACT The Victorians introduced many home improvements including electric lighting, running water and flushing toilets.

Gruesome truth

Only the rich had bathrooms and flushing toilets. The poor lived in crowded slum houses and shared outdoor toilets. Baths were taken in a tub by a coal fire.

Closets and chamber pots

Most houses had **privies** or outdoor toilets that were 'earth closets'. These were small sheds with a seat over a hole in the ground. **Quick lime** was poured in to keep down the smells. A 'night soil man' came to empty them after dark and sold the sewage to farms for fertiliser. During the night, people used **chamber pots** kept under the bed, or commodes (chairs with a chamber pot hidden inside), which they, or their maid servants, had to empty in the morning.

Slums and straw beds

Slum houses were cramped, dirty and damp, and sometimes got flooded with water or sewage from leaking cesspits. Many had rags stuffing holes in the windows. Sometimes, several poor families had to share the same house.

▲ Slum areas were smelly from trades like candle making and bone crushing.

In orphanages and cheap lodgings houses, up to 30 children had to share a room, sleeping on rough rag or straw beds. Some slept on the streets if they had not earned enough pennies during the day to pay for lodgings.

TRUE OR FALSE?
Victorian toothbrushes were made from pigs' bristles.

▲ Children from poor families often had to share the same bed as their parents.

Cruel Rules

FACT Family was very important to the Victorians. Some parents had as many as ten children. Well-off families had comfortable homes and enjoyed **parlour** games and singing round the piano together.

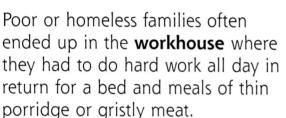
Gruesome truth

Poor or homeless families often ended up in the **workhouse** where they had to do hard work all day in return for a bed and meals of thin porridge or gristly meat.

▼ Workhouse meals were so poor, people sometimes picked scraps of rotten meat off the bones sent for crushing.

▲ Men were housed in separate quarters from women and children.

Workhouses

Families were separated when they got to the workhouse as men, women and children were made to live apart. Lodgings were poor and crowded and people had to do boring jobs like sewing sacks, crushing meat bones or unpicking old rope.

▲ Mothers answered adverts for baby farmers, often meeting in the street to hand over their baby.

Baby farmers

Poor families sometimes suffocated unwanted babies, drowned them or left them on doorsteps or under railway arches. Some were sold to a 'baby farmer'. These women often neglected the child and some secretly drowned them in the river or canal.

Horrid husbands

Victorian women had no vote and few rights. Their husbands owned all their property and could lock them up or beat them without penalty. Children were also seen as the property of their father. He could send them out to work from the age of four and take all their wages for the family.

▲ Husbands were allowed to beat wives with a stick, as long as it was no thicker than their thumb.

Dodgy Dinners

FACT The Victorians invented canned foods, ready meals and kitchen gadgets including cheese graters, potato peelers, pastry cutters and jelly moulds.

Gruesome truth

Victorian dishes included calf's foot jelly, calf ear fritters, pigs' trotters, cods' heads and boiled bullock head, which was served with the brains as a side dish with butter.

Grisly gluttons
The **naturalist** Frank Buckland went further. He wanted to try unusual foods and experimented with dishes of elephant trunk, moles, stewed bluebottles and mice on toast. The Glutton Club also liked experimenting with food and their feasts included dishes of hawk, puma, squirrel and candied maggots.

▲ Victorians cooks used every bit of an animal including the heads and feet.

◀ The surgeon and zoologist Frank Buckland made a hobby of eating all kinds of animals.

Filthy foods

In the early 1900s, there were few laws about food safety. Some bakers and grocers cheated by using cheap and even dangerous ingredients. Chalk and plaster of Paris were added to flour, powdered glass to sugar, and wood shavings to tea. Metals like copper and red lead were sometimes used in butter and bread.

▲ Hygiene was often poor and ice cream could contain lice, beetles and cat and dog hairs!

TRUE OR FALSE?
Victorians used the poison arsenic in cooking.

▲ Some bakers kneaded dough with their unwashed feet!

Dunce Caps and Canes

FACT The Victorians introduced free and compulsory schooling for all children in 1891.

Gruesome truth

Victorian schools could be grim places. It was sometimes so cold in winter that the inkwells froze over. Pupils were punished by being shamed as the **'dunce'** of the class, or beaten by their teacher with a cane.

Cruel classrooms

In Victorian classrooms, children had to sit at desks in rows facing the teacher. Teachers used a whistle to keep the class quiet. If pupils were lazy or got behind with their work, they were made to wear a pointed dunce's cap and stand in the corner of the classroom, facing the wall.

▶ Teachers kept order using harsh corporal punishments.

▼ Some teachers used a springy cane, others a 'tawse' or fringed leather strap, or a 'birch' made from birch twigs.

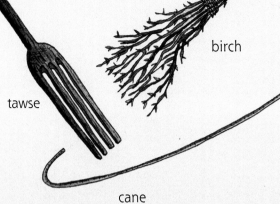

birch

tawse

cane

For bad or naughty behaviour, children were given 'the strap'. This meant beating them across the palms of their hands or on their, sometimes bare, bottoms. If children misbehaved by throwing ink around, they were made to kneel on a hard floor with their hands behind their heads for 20 minutes.

TRUE OR FALSE?

Boys and girls had to enter school through separate doors.

WHAT IS IT?

Arsenic and Leeches

FACT The Victorians made important advances in medicine and surgery including the first **anaesthetics** and **antiseptics**, **sterilised** instruments and surgical masks.

Gruesome truth

In early Victorian times, operations including **amputations** were carried out without anaesthetics. Surgeons did not always wash their hands between operations and just wiped instruments clean. Many patients died from infections or blood poisoning.

▼ Surgeons had no surgical gloves and wore ordinary clothes when operating.

Cruel Crimea

In the 1850s, the nurse Florence Nightingale reported that soldiers wounded in the Crimean War lay in filthy hospitals that were crawling with flies. Limbs that the surgeons had amputated were thrown outside to be eaten by dogs.

► Surgeons often used the same instruments for people and animals.

▲ The same leeches were used over and over again on different patients.

Bad blood

A common remedy was blood-letting. Doctors thought that bleeding a patient would release bad blood that was causing disease. They cut or scratched the patient's skin to make it bleed, then applied a warm cup to draw out the blood. Some patients lost so much blood they fainted. Live leeches were also used to suck blood out of a patient's veins. A drop of blood or milk was applied to encourage the leech to start sucking!

Pongy poultices

Poultices were paste-like mixtures that were applied to wounds, cuts, bites and boils. They could contain anything from goose fat and onions to cow dung!

WHAT IS IT?

'The Great Stink'

FACT The Victorians built drains and underground sewers that we still use today.

Gruesome truth

In early Victorian times, there were no drains or sewers and the river Thames was filthy with rubbish, sewage and even dead bodies.

Dirty water

Many poor people had no running water in their homes and had to fetch water from standpipes in the street or from rivers and wells. Wells were often polluted from nearby cesspits, and dirty drinking water made diseases like **cholera** and **typhoid** common.

The river caused such a great stink in the hot summer of 1858 that the window blinds of the Houses of Parliament had to be sprayed with **quick lime** to keep the smell out.

▶ Newspaper articles and cartoons reported 'The Great Stink' of 1858.

Coal and corpses

Dredger men had the job of fishing dead bodies out of the river. They were paid for every body they found, but many robbed the corpse of any valuables before handing it in! Little children, called Mudlarks, waded into the mud at low tide to scavenge for bits of rope or coal that they could sell for a few pennies.

Mudlarks often went barefoot and got nails or glass in their feet as they scavenged in mud and sewage.

Pea soupers

Cities were also smelly with 'pea soupers', a mixture of fog and smoke from factories and coal fires. Many people suffered with lung and chest diseases from the dirty air.

TRUE OR FALSE?
Early Victorians thought diseases like cholera were spread by smell.

Pickpockets and Pudding Snammers

FACT The Victorian Sir Robert Peel formed the police force in 1829 to fight street crime. Police were called 'bobbies' or 'peelers'.

Gruesome truth

Street crime was common. Children worked in gangs as pickpockets and violent muggers called **garrotters** throttled their victims from behind before stealing their money.

TRUE OR FALSE?
Victorian policemen wore top hats.

◄ River rats stole from bodies drowned in the Thames.

River rats and whizzers

There were so many types of crime they all had special names. 'Whizzers' picked pockets. 'Van draggers' stole from horse-drawn cabs, 'pudding snammers' from bakeries and 'snow droppers' from washing lines. 'River rats' stripped belongings from corpses drowned in the river Thames.

Grisly garrotters

Garrotters were corrupt drivers of London's horse-drawn cabs. They often worked in pairs; one grabbed the victim around the neck and choked him, while the other stole his money.

WHAT IS IT?

▲ Garrotting began in London, then spread to other cities.

Small criminals

Gangs of children worked as pickpockets. Their masters, or 'kidsmen', trained them in the art of picking, or cutting, purses out of pockets. Others slipped through the bars of windows or crawled through drains to get into houses to let burglars in.

◄ Pickpockets often worked in pairs, with one creating a distraction while the other raided the victim's pockets.

Hulks and Hangings

FACT There were strict punishments for crime in Victorian times.

Gruesome truth

Punishments included flogging, public hanging and **transportation** overseas. Even children could be whipped, put in prison, hanged or transported for crimes like theft.

Prison punishments

Victorian prisons were grim places where prisoners had to do hard work like stone breaking or unpicking old rope. Punishments included climbing a treadmill for hours, turning the handle of a heavy **crank** or doing 'shot drill', which meant endlessly passing heavy weights from one to another. If prisoners refused or failed, they could be whipped or put in a **strait jacket** and tied to the wall of their cell.

▼ Treadmills were revolving drums or ladders that prisoners were made to climb for hours on end.

▲ The hulks were crowded, dirty and full of rats.

Horrible hulks

Some prisoners lived on old warships called hulks that were moored on the river Thames. The prisoners wore heavy leg irons while on board. In day time, they were sent out to do hard work like clearing sewers or stone breaking.

◀ The Gloucester Hangman was famous for entertaining the crowds by shaking the corpse's hand or twirling the body round.

Public hangings

Public hangings went on until 1868. Crowds gathered to watch the criminal swing from the rope. Some picnicked by the **gallows** and there was often singing, drunkenness and fighting among the spectators. Rich people sometimes rented houses nearby to get a good view.

WHAT IS IT?

Transportation

Serious criminals were transported to Australia for up to 14 years of hard work. One in a hundred died on the 5-month sea journey. Children could be transported just for stealing a loaf of bread.

Foul Factories and Monstrous Mills

FACT Steam-powered machinery in Victorian mills and factories produced more goods faster than ever before.

Gruesome truth

Factory and mill workers, including children as young as six, worked long hours doing hard, and sometimes dangerous, work.

Dust and danger

Factories and mills were noisy, dusty and dangerous places. Mill workers often had accidents and lost fingers or hands, went deaf from the noise of machinery or suffered burns or lung diseases. There was no **compensation** for injuries at work. They could be fined for laziness or even just talking on the job. Some factory owners cheated them by setting clocks late then fining the workers for turning up late.

▶ In the potteries, children had to carry heavy loads of wet clay on their heads.

Child labour

In the cotton mills, small children had to scramble under moving machinery to oil the parts or clean up fluff. If they were lazy or fell asleep, some cruel masters punished them by beating them with ropes or iron sticks, throwing them into cold water or hanging them up by their feet.

▶ Little children were small enough to squeeze under machinery.

Phossy jaw

Girls who worked in the match factories suffered from a disease called 'phossy jaw'. This was caused by fumes from the chemical phosphorus which ate away their jaw bones.

◀ A match girl's skull showing the damage to her jaw.

WHAT IS IT?

Chimneys and Coalmines

FACT In Victorian times, coal from the mines powered factories, steam ships and trains, as well as heating and cooking in homes.

Gruesome truth

Mine owners employed small children to work in underground tunnels that were too small for ponies.

▼ Many tunnels were so small children could not stand up in them.

Hurriers and trappers

Children had to crawl on their hands and knees in dark, damp tunnels. **Hurriers** dragged or pushed heavy coal carts, which were fixed by chains to their belts. **Trappers** had to sit all day in a tunnel opening the doors when the carts came through. Sometimes rats stole their bread and cheese. Many children were bullied and beaten by their masters and got injured or killed in accidents or explosions.

Chummy boys

Coal fires heated Victorian houses. Chimney sweeps sent small boys up the chimneys to clean out the soot. The 'chummy boys' slept on bags of soot and were fed on greasy soups and fatty meat. Their masters rubbed salt into their skin to toughen them up and beat them to punish them.

Many boys suffered lung diseases from breathing in the soot and fumes. Others died in falls or got stuck in chimney bends.

▲ Chimney sweeps stood below the chummy boys, sticking pins in their feet or burning straw to stop them coming down before the job was done.

Boxing and Baiting

FACT The Victorians enjoyed many kinds of spectator sport.

Gruesome truth

Popular spectator sports included cock fighting, dog fighting and badger baiting. Even after they were banned in 1835, they carried on illegally, especially in country areas.

Animal baiting

Cockerels were specially bred and trained for fighting. Dogs were also trained to fight each other and for the sport of ratting, which remained legal. At one time there were more than 70 rat pits in London. They were often in beer houses where publicans sold rats for three pence and people gambled on the results. Rat catchers were paid to supply the rats. Dozens of rats were released into a pit then a terrier was put in to chase and kill them. The bets were on how many he could kill in sixty seconds.

▲ Cockerels were fitted with brass spurs tied on with leather straps. They were sharp enough to kill.

▶ Sometimes there were up to 100 rats in a pit.

Boxers and brawls

Another popular spectator sport was boxing. Boxers fought bare knuckle (without protective gloves). Often fights descended into wrestling and brawling and the police had to be called in to break them up. Football was becoming popular but, without proper rules, it was a rough game and there were frequent injuries.

▼ Women took part in boxing, which had few rules other than not kicking an opponent when they were down on the ground!

Terriers were also used for badger baiting. The badger was put into a box with a tunnel-like entrance then a dog was sent in after it.

WHAT IS IT?

Freaks and Acrobats

FACT The Victorians enjoyed all kinds of entertainment, from theatrical plays and horse racing to travelling circuses and street shows.

Gruesome truth

Freak shows were popular. They travelled around the country, displaying anyone who was different as a spectacle for crowds to gawp at. Dwarves, giants, people who had lost, or been born without, limbs, **conjoined twins** and bearded ladies all appeared in the freak shows.

▼ Freak shows paraded characters on stage or charged for a peep through a curtain or screen. Some famous characters were fakes like the Hairy Man of Borneo who was really a monkey!

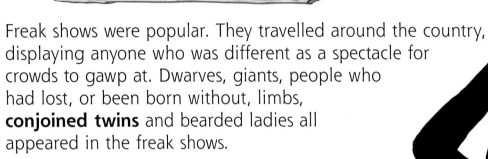

◀ Some children were trained to become street tumblers or circus acrobats. Their masters sometimes strapped them up to make their legs and arms more bendy!

Melodrama and murders

At the theatre, the Victorians loved plays full of blood and murder. The crowds were often rowdy, booing, hissing and jeering at the actors.

Monstrous museums

Victorian museums could be gruesome places. The Anatomy Museum displayed waxwork models of diseased flesh and body parts. Natural history collections included the stuffed bodies of deformed baby animals, like a kitten born with eight legs or a calf born with two heads.

▲ Deformed animals were stuffed and put on display in museums.

# Glossary

amputations	Cutting off diseased or damaged parts of the body.
anaesthetics	Substances that cause temporary loss of consciousness.
antiseptics	Substances that clean and sterilise wounds.
birch	A spray of birch twigs used to beat a child.
chamber pots	China or enamel pots kept under the bed for weeing into.
cholera	An infection in the intestine, often caused by drinking dirty water.
compensation	Money paid to make up for a wrong.
conjoined twins	Twins born joined together.
crank	A heavy drum which was turned by a handle.
dunce	A pupil who may not be very clever.
gallows	A wooden frame used for hanging people.
garrotters	Criminals who throttled people then mugged them.
hurriers	Children who had to haul the coal carts in Victorian coal mines.
naturalist	A person who studies natural history.
parlour	A formal living room for entertaining.
privies	Outside toilets, often built at the bottom of gardens.
quick lime	A chemical compound made from calcium.
sterilised	Clean and free from germs.
strait jacket	A stiff jacket which binds the arms to the body.
tawse	A leather strap used to beat a child.
transportation	Sent to a far-away country for committing a crime.
trappers	Children who had to open the doors in the coal tunnels.
typhoid	An infection in the intestine, often caused by drinking dirty water.
workhouse	A place where the homeless were sent to live in Victorian times.

 # Further Information

Books

Avoid being a Victorian Servant
by Fiona MacDonald (Book House, 2005)

The Vile Victorians (Horrible Histories) by Terry
Deary and Martin Brown (Scholastic, 2007))

The Worst Children's Jobs in History
by Tony Robinson (Macmillan, 2005)

You Wouldn't Want to Be a Victorian Miner by
John Malam (Wayland, 2002)

*You Wouldn't Want to Be a Victorian School
child* by John Malam (Wayland, 2002)

Websites

www.bbc.co.uk/schools/victorians
www.victorians.org.uk
www.woodlands-junior.kent.sch.uk/
Homework/Victorians.html

Places to visit

Beamish Museum, County Durham
Ironbridge Gorge Museum, Telford,
Shropshire
Ragged School Museum, London

 # Illustrator Note

The Victorian age brought great changes
to the world as well as ordinary people.
New inventions like the flushing toilet, the
phone and the great age of steam power
helped everyday lives. However, looking
back in time through this book, it is clear
to see that change also meant very hard
work, and in many ways led to a very
gruesome life.

Matt Buckingham

Index

Numbers in **bold** refer
to illustrations.

Answers

Page 7 True or false? True

Page 11 True or false? False: but some ingredients contained lead, which is poisonous.

Page 13 What is it? A back straightener. Some pupils were made to wear these to make them sit or stand upright.

Page 13 True or false? True.

Page 15 What is it? A leech jar

Page 17 True or false? True: it was called the miasmic theory.

Page 18 True or false? True

Page 19 What is it? A leather neck guard for protection against attack by a garrotter

Page 21 What is it? A crank. The drum was full of sand to make it heavy but prisoners could be forced to turn it up to 10,000 times.

Page 23 What is it? 'A cat', a rope with four tails used by supervisors to discipline child workers in Victorian mills.

Page 27 What is it? A pair of Victorian cock-fighting spurs with a stone for sharpening them.

The Gruesome Truth About

Contents of titles in the series:

The Middle Ages
978 0 7502 6133 3
The Marvellous Middle Ages
Dingy Dwellings
Herbs and hygiene
Weary workers
Working children
Boars and bustards
Hunting and hawks
Castles and Catapults
Sheriffs and Stocks
Terrible tortures
Deadly diseases
Curious cures
Prayers and Pardons

The Tudors
978 0 7502 6134 0
The Terrific Tudors
Tudor Grooming
Pongs and Pomanders
Spit roasts and sparrows
Cock fights and cudgels
Cruel classrooms
Scary Surgery
The Plague
Sailors and Explorers
Men and Muskets
Crime and Punishment
Terrible Tortures
Women and Witches

The Victorians
978 0 7502 6135 7
The Vivacious Victorians
Homes and Hygiene
Cruel Rules
Dodgy Dinners
Dunce Caps and Canes
Arsenic and Leeches
'The Great Stink'
Pickpockets and Pudding Snammers
Hulks and Hangings
Foul Factories and Monstrous Mills
Chimneys and Coalmines
Boxing and Baiting
Freaks and Acrobats

The Vikings
978 0 7502 6132 6
The Valiant Vikings
Ruthless Raiders
Wild Warriors
Sacrifices and Sagas
Chieftains and Slaves
Laws and 'Things'
Families and Feuds
Smoky Homes
Soap and Steam Baths
Horrid Hunters
Seabirds and Sausages
Cruel Competitors
Pyres, Fires and Funerals

WAYLAND